Embracing Calm: A Guide to Mana~~~~ ~~~~

Table of Contents

Introduction

3

Embracing Calm: A Guide to Managing Anxiety

A Note from the Author

Anxiety is a common and understandable reaction to the challenges and uncertainties of life. But if left unchecked, it can become overwhelming, affecting your daily life and well-being. The good news is that you have the power to manage and even conquer anxiety.

In this eBook, we will embark on a journey together to explore anxiety, its triggers, and the proven strategies that can help you regain control of your life. I've poured my heart and soul into providing you with practical, easy-to-understand advice that you can start implementing today.

Anxiety can be a formidable adversary, but with the right tools and mindset, you can embrace calm and reclaim your life. This eBook is your guide, your companion, and your source of hope. Let's begin this journey toward a more peaceful, fulfilling existence—one step at a time.

-Ren H.

Embracing Calm: A Guide to Managing Anxiety

Dear Reader,

Welcome to "Embracing Calm: A Guide to Managing Anxiety." I'm truly honored to be your guide on this journey towards a life of greater peace and serenity. In these pages, we'll embark on a heartfelt exploration of anxiety—an all-too-common companion in today's fast-paced world. But fear not, for you are not alone, and together, we will learn how to tame this relentless beast.

Acknowledging Anxiety

Anxiety. It's a word that carries a weight of emotions, thoughts, and experiences. It's a word that millions of people, from all walks of life, can relate to. Perhaps you're reading this because anxiety has been a constant presence in your life, casting a shadow over your everyday moments. Maybe you've experienced that relentless pounding of your heart, those racing thoughts that seem impossible to quiet, or that knot in your stomach that refuses to loosen its grip.

It's crucial to recognize that anxiety is not a sign of weakness or inadequacy. It's a natural response to the challenges and uncertainties that life throws our way. Yet, when anxiety becomes overwhelming, it can feel like an insurmountable mountain. That's why we're here—to acknowledge anxiety, to face it head-on, and to learn how to manage it.

The Path to Inner Peace

Our journey towards managing anxiety isn't just about reducing its presence; it's also about finding inner peace. It's about discovering that even in the midst of life's chaos, you can experience moments of tranquility and calm. It's about learning to be kind to yourself, to recognize your own strength, and to embrace a life free from the shackles of anxiety.

Embracing Calm: A Guide to Managing Anxiety

How this eBook can help

You might be wondering, "How can this eBook possibly help me manage my anxiety?" The answer lies in its pages. Within these chapters, you'll find a wealth of information, strategies, and practical advice that can be tailored to your unique experience. It's not a one-size-fits-all solution, but rather a toolkit from which you can draw the tools that resonate most with you.

You'll discover a wide range of strategies, from deep breathing techniques and mindfulness meditation to cognitive restructuring and building resilience. We'll explore the power of your thoughts and how to challenge those negative patterns that fuel anxiety. You'll also find guidance on seeking professional help when needed and how to navigate anxiety in various aspects of your life—whether it's at work, in relationships, or while parenting.

This eBook is a comprehensive resource that combines scientific insights with real-world wisdom. It's not just about managing anxiety; it's about transforming your relationship with it. Together, we'll build a personalized action plan that suits your needs and empowers you to take back control of your life.

But beyond strategies and techniques, this eBook is also about understanding and compassion. It's a reminder that you are not alone in your journey. Many have walked this path before you, and their stories and experiences will accompany you along the way. You'll find inspirational quotes, journaling prompts, and additional resources to enrich your learning.

So, dear reader, as we embark on this journey together, know that you are taking a courageous step towards a life of greater calm and contentment. Anxiety may have been your constant companion, but it doesn't have to be the author of your life story. Let's embrace calm, one chapter at a time, and work towards a brighter, more peaceful tomorrow.

Embracing Calm: A Guide to Managing Anxiety

Chapter 1: Understanding Anxiety

Welcome to the first chapter of our journey together, where we'll delve into the heart of anxiety—what it is, how it manifests, and why it's an essential starting point on our path to embracing calm. It's my sincere hope that by the end of this chapter, you'll have a clearer understanding of anxiety, recognizing it not as an adversary to be feared but as a part of your experience that we'll learn to navigate together.

What Is Anxiety?

Anxiety is a natural human emotion, an integral part of our survival mechanism. It's the "fight or flight" response that kept our ancestors safe in the face of life-threatening situations. When faced with danger, the body releases adrenaline, heightening alertness and preparing for action. This response can be lifesaving in critical moments.

However, in today's world, the triggers for anxiety often differ from those faced by our ancestors. Modern life presents a barrage of stressors—work pressure, financial concerns, relationship challenges, and health worries—that can set off the same physiological response. When anxiety becomes chronic, it can have a profound impact on our physical and mental well-being.

Types of Anxiety Disorders

Anxiety isn't a one-size-fits-all experience. There's a spectrum of anxiety disorders, each with its unique characteristics:

- **Generalized Anxiety Disorder (GAD):** This type of anxiety involves excessive worry and fear about everyday events or activities. People with GAD often find it challenging to control their anxiety, and it can interfere with their daily lives.

- **Social Anxiety Disorder:** Social anxiety is an intense fear of social situations, leading to avoidance of social interactions. It can manifest as fear of public speaking, meeting new people, or attending social events.

- **Panic Disorder:** Panic disorder is characterized by recurring, unexpected panic attacks, which are intense episodes of fear and physical symptoms like heart palpitations, sweating, and trembling.

- **Specific Phobias:** These are irrational fears of specific objects or situations, such as heights, spiders, or flying. When exposed to their phobia, individuals may experience extreme anxiety.

- **Obsessive-Compulsive Disorder (OCD):** OCD involves intrusive, distressing thoughts (obsessions) that lead to repetitive behaviors or mental acts (compulsions) aimed at reducing anxiety.

- **Post-Traumatic Stress Disorder (PTSD):** PTSD can develop after experiencing a traumatic event. It's characterized by flashbacks, nightmares, and severe anxiety related to the trauma.

- **Separation Anxiety Disorder:** Primarily seen in children, this disorder involves excessive fear or anxiety about separation from caregivers.

- **Agoraphobia:** Agoraphobia is a fear of being in situations where escape might be difficult, leading to avoidance of places or situations like crowded places, public transportation, or open spaces.

Understanding the specific type of anxiety you're dealing with can help tailor your approach to managing it. But regardless of the specific diagnosis, the strategies we'll explore in this eBook can be valuable for managing anxiety in its various forms.

The Science behind Anxiety

Anxiety is not merely a state of mind; it's a complex interplay of thoughts, emotions, and physiological responses. Understanding the science behind anxiety can help demystify it and offer you insights into how to manage it effectively.

The Amygdala: At the heart of the brain's emotional processing is the amygdala, a tiny, almond-shaped structure. It's responsible for detecting potential threats in our environment and initiating the "fight or flight" response. When the amygdala perceives danger, it sends signals to the rest of the brain and body, triggering a cascade of physiological changes.

The Stress Hormone: The amygdala's alarm signal prompts the release of stress hormones, primarily cortisol and adrenaline. These hormones prepare the body to face a threat by increasing heart rate, dilating airways, and redirecting blood flow to muscles.

The Cognitive Component: Anxiety is not limited to physiological responses. It also involves cognitive components—our thoughts and interpretations of situations. When anxiety takes hold, our thoughts often become skewed toward negative and catastrophic outcomes.

Embracing Calm: A Guide to Managing Anxiety

The Vicious Cycle: This combination of physiological and cognitive factors can create a vicious cycle. An anxious thought triggers a stress response, which, in turn, reinforces the anxious thought. Breaking this cycle is a key aspect of managing anxiety effectively.

Recognizing that anxiety is a multi-faceted experience, encompassing both physical and mental aspects, is a crucial step toward understanding and addressing it.

Anxiety vs. Stress

Before we delve further into anxiety, let's briefly distinguish between anxiety and stress, as these terms are often used interchangeably.

Stress is a natural response to external pressures or demands. It can be beneficial in small doses, motivating us to meet deadlines or respond to challenges. However, chronic stress can lead to physical and mental health issues.

Anxiety, on the other hand, often involves excessive worry or fear about future events, situations, or potential dangers. While stress typically relates to specific stressors, anxiety often lacks a clear cause or can be triggered by everyday situations.

The key distinction is that stress is a reaction to a particular stressor, whereas anxiety often lacks a specific trigger or is out of proportion to the situation. Both stress and anxiety can coexist, and the strategies we'll explore in this eBook can be beneficial for managing both.

In this opening chapter, we've laid the foundation for our journey. You now have a clearer understanding of what anxiety is, the different types of anxiety disorders, the science behind anxiety, and how it differs from stress. Remember, you're not alone in this journey. Anxiety is a common human experience, and countless individuals have successfully learned to manage it. As we continue, we'll explore practical strategies and insights to help you take the first steps toward embracing calm in your life.

Chapter 2: Recognizing Anxiety Triggers

In the previous chapter, we delved into the fundamental aspects of anxiety, seeking to understand its nature and various forms. Now, as we continue our journey toward embracing calm, we'll shine a light on a crucial aspect of managing anxiety—recognizing its triggers. By identifying these triggers, we can take significant steps toward gaining control over our anxious responses and developing effective strategies for managing them.

Identifying Personal Triggers

Anxiety triggers are the catalysts that set off feelings of unease, fear, or worry. They vary widely from person to person, and recognizing your unique triggers is an essential step in managing anxiety effectively. Here's how to begin identifying your personal triggers:

Self-Reflection: Take some time for introspection. Reflect on situations, thoughts, or events that consistently lead to increased anxiety. What were you doing, thinking, or feeling when anxiety surged?

Emotional Awareness: Pay attention to your emotional responses throughout the day. When you experience anxiety, take note of the circumstances and emotions surrounding it.

Keep a Journal: Consider keeping an anxiety journal. Record instances of heightened anxiety, describing what happened, how you felt, and any thoughts that crossed your mind. Over time, patterns may emerge.

Common Anxiety Triggers

While personal triggers can vary widely, several common anxiety triggers are prevalent among individuals. These include:

Embracing Calm: A Guide to Managing Anxiety

1. Uncertainty: The unpredictability of life can be a significant source of anxiety. It's natural to want stability and control, but the reality is that uncertainty is a constant companion.

2. Social Situations: For some, social interactions can be anxiety-inducing. Whether it's speaking in public, meeting new people, or attending social events, these situations can trigger social anxiety.

3. Health Worries: Concerns about one's health or the health of loved ones can lead to heightened anxiety. The fear of illness or a medical condition can be a powerful trigger.

4. Work Pressure: The demands of the workplace, deadlines, and job-related stressors can significantly contribute to anxiety. Balancing work responsibilities can be a challenge.

5. Financial Concerns: Money-related worries, such as debt, financial instability, or the fear of unexpected expenses, are common triggers for anxiety.

6. Relationships: Difficulties in relationships, conflicts, or the fear of abandonment can lead to relationship anxiety.

7. Major Life Changes: Significant life events, such as moving, getting married, having a child, or experiencing a loss, can trigger anxiety as we navigate these transitions.

Understanding these common triggers can help you begin to recognize potential sources of anxiety in your life. It's important to note that some triggers may overlap or lead to a cascade of anxiety. For example, financial concerns can impact work performance, which, in turn, affects relationships.

Embracing Calm: A Guide to Managing Anxiety

The Mind-Body Connection

Anxiety is not solely a mental experience—it's deeply intertwined with our physical well-being. Recognizing the mind-body connection can be a powerful tool in understanding and managing anxiety triggers.

Physical Responses: Anxiety often triggers physical sensations such as rapid heartbeat, sweating, muscle tension, and digestive discomfort. These physical responses can intensify the feeling of anxiety.

Stress and Anxiety: Chronic stress can lower our threshold for anxiety triggers. When we're stressed, even minor stressors can provoke heightened anxiety.

Self-Care and Well-Being: Engaging in self-care practices such as regular exercise, a balanced diet, and adequate sleep can help reduce physical vulnerabilities to anxiety.

By being attuned to your body's responses and making choices that promote physical well-being, you can build resilience against anxiety triggers.

Journaling for Awareness

One effective way to gain insight into your anxiety triggers is through journaling. Keeping a journal allows you to document your thoughts, emotions, and the circumstances surrounding anxiety episodes. Here's how to use journaling for self-awareness:

Create a Journal: Choose a notebook or a digital platform to serve as your anxiety journal.

Document Triggers: When you experience anxiety, write down the date, time, and the triggering situation or thought. Describe your emotional state and any physical sensations.

Patterns and Insights: Over time, review your journal entries for patterns. Are there recurring triggers? Do certain situations or thoughts consistently lead to anxiety?

Reflect and Plan: Use your journal as a tool for reflection. What insights have you gained? Are there specific triggers you'd like to address or strategies you'd like to try?

Emotional Release: Writing can also serve as an emotional release. Expressing your thoughts and feelings on paper can provide a sense of relief.

As you become more aware of your anxiety triggers, you'll be better equipped to manage them. Recognizing triggers is a significant step, but it's just the beginning of our journey toward embracing calm.

In this chapter, we've explored the critical concept of recognizing anxiety triggers. By identifying these catalysts, you've taken a proactive step in understanding your anxiety better. In the chapters to come, we'll delve into practical strategies for managing anxiety, helping you build a toolkit for navigating life's challenges with greater ease and resilience. Remember, you're not alone in this journey, and with each step, you're moving closer to a life of peace and well-being.

Embracing Calm: A Guide to Managing Anxiety

Chapter 3: Proven Strategies for Managing Anxiety

As we continue our journey toward embracing calm, we arrive at a pivotal chapter—where we dive into practical strategies for managing anxiety. The journey ahead holds the promise of greater peace, resilience, and a newfound sense of control over the anxiety that may have felt overpowering. These strategies, while simple to understand, have the power to transform the way you respond to anxiety triggers.

Breathing Techniques

Let's begin with one of the most accessible and effective tools for managing anxiety: breathing techniques. Your breath is a powerful anchor to the present moment and can serve as a calming force in times of distress. Here's a simple technique to get you started:

The 4-7-8 Technique:

1. Find a quiet place to sit or lie down.

2. Close your eyes and take a deep breath in through your nose for a count of 4 seconds.

3. Hold your breath for a count of 7 seconds.

4. Exhale slowly and completely through your mouth for a count of 8 seconds.

5. Repeat this cycle for a few minutes, focusing on the rhythm of your breath.

This technique helps slow down your heart rate and activates the body's relaxation response. Practice it regularly, especially when you notice anxiety creeping in.

Embracing Calm: A Guide to Managing Anxiety

Mindfulness Meditation

Mindfulness meditation is a practice that cultivates your ability to stay present and nonjudgmentally aware of your thoughts and sensations. It's an invaluable tool for managing anxiety. Here's how to get started:

Find a Quiet Space: Choose a comfortable, quiet place where you won't be disturbed.

Sit Comfortably: Sit in a relaxed but alert posture. You can also lie down if you prefer.

Focus on Your Breath: Pay attention to your breath as you inhale and exhale. Notice the rise and fall of your chest or the sensation of air passing through your nostrils.

Acknowledge Thoughts: When your mind inevitably wanders, as it often does, gently bring your focus back to your breath. Don't judge yourself for wandering thoughts; it's entirely natural.

Start with Short Sessions: Begin with just a few minutes of meditation each day, gradually increasing the duration as you become more comfortable with the practice.

Mindfulness meditation can help you become more aware of the thoughts and sensations that accompany anxiety. Over time, it can provide a sense of inner calm and greater control over your reactions.

Progressive Muscle Relaxation

Anxiety often manifests in physical tension, such as tight muscles and clenched jaws. Progressive muscle relaxation is a technique that can help you release this physical tension. Here's how it works:

Find a Quiet Space: As with meditation, select a quiet, comfortable place to practice.

Embracing Calm: A Guide to Managing Anxiety

Start from Head to Toe: Begin at your head and work your way down through your body. Tense each muscle group for a few seconds and then release it. Pay attention to the sensations of tension and relaxation.

Breathe: Remember to breathe deeply and slowly as you go through each muscle group.

Visualize: As you relax each muscle group, visualize the tension melting away and being replaced by a sense of calm.

Repeat as Needed: You can repeat this process as many times as necessary to release tension and reduce anxiety.

Grounding Exercises

Grounding exercises are particularly useful when you're experiencing heightened anxiety or panic. They help anchor you to the present moment and alleviate feelings of detachment or disorientation. Here's a simple grounding exercise:

5-4-3-2-1 Technique:

1. Identify and describe five things you can see around you.

2. Focus on four things you can touch or physically feel.

3. Acknowledge three things you can hear, whether they're distant sounds or those nearby.

4. Notice two things you can smell, whether pleasant or neutral.

5. Lastly, taste something or acknowledge one thing you could taste if you were to eat or drink it.

This exercise engages your senses and brings you back to the here and now, reducing the grip of anxiety.

These four techniques—breathing, mindfulness meditation, progressive muscle relaxation, and grounding exercises—are valuable tools you can integrate into your daily life to manage anxiety effectively. Remember that practice is key. The more you incorporate these techniques into your routine, the more naturally they will come to you in moments of anxiety.

In the next chapter, we'll explore the power of your thoughts and how to challenge negative thinking patterns that can exacerbate anxiety. Your journey to embracing calm continues, and with each step, you're building a foundation of resilience and well-being.

Chapter 4: The Power of Your Thoughts

Welcome to another chapter of our journey towards managing anxiety and embracing a life of greater calm. In this chapter, we'll explore the profound impact your thoughts have on your anxiety and overall well-being. By understanding the power of your thoughts and learning how to challenge negative thinking patterns, you can take significant strides toward managing anxiety effectively.

Cognitive Distortions

Our minds are powerful storytellers, but sometimes, they can tell us stories that aren't entirely accurate. These distorted thought patterns, known as cognitive distortions, can exacerbate anxiety. Recognizing and addressing them is a crucial step in managing anxiety. Here are some common cognitive distortions:

1. Catastrophizing: This distortion involves jumping to the worst-case scenario. For example, if you make a mistake at work, you might immediately think, "I'm going to get fired."

2. All-or-Nothing Thinking: This distortion is characterized by extreme thinking—seeing situations as all good or all bad, with no middle ground. If you didn't complete your entire to-do list, you might think, "I'm a total failure."

3. Mind Reading: Assuming you know what others are thinking and believing they have negative opinions about you. For instance, if someone doesn't respond to your message, you might think, "They must be angry with me."

4. Personalization: Taking responsibility for events that are beyond your control. If a friend cancels plans, you might think, "They canceled because of something I did."

5. Overgeneralization: Drawing broad conclusions based on limited evidence. If one job interview goes poorly, you might conclude, "I'm terrible at interviews, and I'll never get a job."

6. Emotional Reasoning: Believing that your emotions reflect reality. If you feel anxious, you might think, "I must be in real danger."

Challenging Negative Thoughts

Now that we've identified these cognitive distortions, let's explore strategies for challenging and reframing negative thoughts. This is a powerful tool for managing anxiety:

1. Recognize the Distortion: When you notice a negative thought, pause and identify the distortion at play. Ask yourself, "Is this thought based on facts, or is it a distortion?"

2. Gather Evidence: Examine the evidence for and against your negative thought. Are there objective reasons to support it, or is it based on assumptions?

3. Consider Alternative Interpretations: Explore alternative, more balanced ways of thinking about the situation. For example, instead of thinking, "I'm a total failure," you might consider, "I didn't complete everything on my to-do list, but I did accomplish some important tasks."

4. Practice Self-Compassion: Be kind to yourself. Remember that everyone makes mistakes and faces challenges. Treat yourself with the same compassion and understanding you would offer a friend in a similar situation.

Affirmations for Anxiety

Affirmations are positive statements that can counteract negative thoughts and promote a more optimistic mindset. They're a valuable tool for managing anxiety and boosting self-esteem. Here are some anxiety-affirmations to consider:

Embracing Calm: A Guide to Managing Anxiety

1. "I am in control of my thoughts and emotions." Remind yourself that you have the power to influence your mental state.

2. "I am resilient and capable of facing challenges." Reinforce your inner strength and ability to overcome difficulties.

3. "I choose to focus on the present moment." Encourage mindfulness and present-moment awareness.

4. "I am worthy of love, happiness, and peace." Remind yourself of your inherent worthiness.

5. "I release my attachment to things beyond my control." Let go of the need to control every aspect of life.

6. "I am surrounded by support and love." Acknowledge the presence of a support system, whether it's friends, family, or professionals.

7. "I am resilient and capable of adapting to change." Embrace change as an opportunity for growth.

Affirmations are most effective when repeated regularly and believed. Choose affirmations that resonate with you personally, and incorporate them into your daily routine.

By understanding and challenging negative thinking patterns, you gain a powerful tool for managing anxiety. Remember that changing thought patterns takes practice, but over time, it can lead to a profound shift in how you respond to anxiety triggers.

In the next chapter, we'll explore the concept of building resilience—a key factor in effectively managing anxiety. Your journey continues, and with each step, you're moving closer to a life of peace and well-being.

Embracing Calm: A Guide to Managing Anxiety

Chapter 5: Building Resilience

Welcome to another chapter of our journey towards managing anxiety and fostering a life of greater calm. In this chapter, we will explore the concept of resilience—a vital attribute that can help you face life's challenges with grace and fortitude. By understanding how to build resilience, you can develop a powerful ally in your quest to manage anxiety effectively.

Nutrition and Anxiety

It may surprise you to learn that what you eat can influence your anxiety levels. Nutrition plays a crucial role in maintaining mental and emotional well-being. Here's how you can make food choices that support anxiety management:

Balanced Diet: Ensure that your diet includes a variety of foods, with an emphasis on fruits, vegetables, whole grains, lean proteins, and healthy fats. Avoid excessive consumption of sugary or highly processed foods, which can lead to energy spikes and crashes, affecting mood.

Hydration: Stay adequately hydrated throughout the day. Dehydration can lead to feelings of fatigue and irritability, which can exacerbate anxiety.

Caffeine and Alcohol: Be mindful of your caffeine and alcohol intake. Both substances can affect sleep and anxiety levels. Consider reducing or eliminating them if you notice they contribute to your anxiety.

Regular Meals: Maintain a regular eating schedule to stabilize blood sugar levels. Skipping meals can lead to irritability and increased anxiety.

Embracing Calm: A Guide to Managing Anxiety

Exercise for Mind and Body

Physical activity is a potent tool for managing anxiety. Regular exercise can improve mood, reduce stress, and boost overall well-being. Here's how to incorporate exercise into your routine:

Choose Activities You Enjoy: Find physical activities you genuinely enjoy, whether it's walking, dancing, yoga, or swimming. When you enjoy what you're doing, exercise becomes a rewarding part of your day.

Set Realistic Goals: Start with achievable fitness goals and gradually increase intensity and duration. Consistency is more important than intensity.

Mind-Body Practices: Mindfulness-based activities like yoga and tai chi not only provide physical benefits but also promote relaxation and mental clarity.

The Importance of Sleep

Quality sleep is a cornerstone of mental health and resilience. Lack of sleep can exacerbate anxiety symptoms. Here are some strategies for improving your sleep:

Establish a Routine: Try to go to bed and wake up at the same times each day, even on weekends. This helps regulate your body's internal clock.

Create a Relaxing Bedtime Ritual: Engage in calming activities before bedtime, such as reading, gentle stretching, or practicing deep breathing exercises.

Limit Screen Time: Reduce exposure to screens (phones, tablets, computers, TVs) before bedtime, as the blue light emitted can interfere with sleep.

Create a Comfortable Sleep Environment: Ensure your bedroom is conducive to sleep, with a comfortable mattress and adequate room darkening.

The Role of Social Support

Strong social connections are a significant source of resilience. Building and maintaining relationships can help you navigate life's challenges. Here's how you can nurture your social support network:

Reach Out: Don't hesitate to reach out to friends, family, or support groups when you need to talk or share your feelings. Social connections can provide comfort and understanding.

Set Boundaries: It's essential to set healthy boundaries in relationships. This means communicating your needs and respecting the boundaries of others.

Seek Professional Help: If anxiety is affecting your relationships, consider seeking the guidance of a therapist or counselor who can help you navigate interpersonal challenges.

The Mind-Body Connection

The mind and body are intricately connected, and taking care of your physical health can have a profound impact on your mental well-being. By prioritizing nutrition, exercise, sleep, and social connections, you're fortifying yourself against the negative effects of anxiety.

As you embark on your journey to build resilience, remember that progress takes time. Small, consistent steps can lead to significant changes in your overall well-being. In the next chapter, we'll explore practical coping mechanisms that you can use when anxiety strikes. Your journey towards embracing calm continues, and with each step, you're cultivating greater resilience.

Chapter 6: Coping with Anxiety in Real Time

In this chapter, we'll explore practical coping mechanisms that you can employ when anxiety strikes. Life can be unpredictable, and anxiety may surface at unexpected moments. By having a toolkit of strategies at your disposal, you can navigate these challenging moments with greater ease and resilience.

Grounding Techniques

Grounding techniques are invaluable when you're experiencing acute anxiety or panic. They help anchor you to the present moment, providing a sense of stability and control. Here are a few grounding techniques to consider:

1. 5-4-3-2-1 Technique: We introduced this technique in a previous chapter. It involves engaging your senses by identifying and describing specific things you see, touch, hear, smell, and potentially taste in your immediate environment.

2. Belly Breathing: Focus on your breath by taking slow, deep breaths, making sure your abdomen rises and falls with each breath. This technique helps counteract shallow, rapid breathing associated with anxiety.

3. Progressive Muscle Relaxation: We also discussed this technique earlier. Tense and then relax different muscle groups in your body, starting from your toes and working your way up to your head.

4. Mindful Observation: Choose an object in your surroundings and observe it closely, paying attention to its shape, color, texture, and any details you might not have noticed before.

Embracing Calm: A Guide to Managing Anxiety

Positive Self-Talk

The way you talk to yourself during moments of anxiety can make a significant difference in how you feel. Replace negative self-talk with more positive and compassionate language:

1. Challenge Negative Thoughts: When you notice negative or catastrophic thoughts, challenge them. Ask yourself, "Is this thought based on facts? What's the evidence against it?"

2. Self-Compassion: Be kind and understanding toward yourself. Treat yourself as you would treat a friend facing a similar situation. Remind yourself that it's okay to feel anxious at times.

3. Affirmations: Continue using positive affirmations, reinforcing your resilience and ability to manage anxiety.

4. Reframe Fearful Language: Instead of saying, "I can't handle this," try saying, "I can manage this moment by moment."

Mindfulness and Distraction

Mindfulness practices can help you stay present and reduce the intensity of anxiety. Consider these approaches:

1. Mindful Breathing: Focus on your breath, noting each inhale and exhale. When your mind wanders, gently bring your focus back to your breath.

2. Grounding in the Present: Use the 5-4-3-2-1 technique or other grounding exercises to bring your attention to the here and now.

3. Guided Imagery: Visualize a calming and peaceful place, such as a beach or a forest. Imagine yourself there, engaging all your senses in the experience.

4. Distraction Techniques: Engage in activities that require your full attention, such as solving puzzles, drawing, or playing a musical instrument. Distraction can be an effective way to redirect your focus away from anxiety.

The Importance of Acceptance

Acceptance is a fundamental component of managing anxiety. It doesn't mean resigning yourself to a life of anxiety but acknowledging that it's a part of your experience. Here's how to practice acceptance:

1. Validate Your Feelings: Recognize that it's okay to feel anxious at times. Emotions are a natural part of being human.

2. Avoid Judgment: Refrain from judging yourself for experiencing anxiety. Self-judgment only adds to the burden of anxiety.

3. Surrender Control: Understand that there are things beyond your control, and that's okay. Trying to control everything can increase anxiety.

4. Focus on What You Can Control: While you can't control everything, you can control your response to anxiety. This includes the coping strategies you choose to employ.

Seeking Professional Help

If anxiety becomes overwhelming or significantly impairs your daily life, don't hesitate to seek professional help. A therapist or counselor can provide guidance and support tailored to your specific needs.

The Journey Continues

As you explore these coping mechanisms, remember that managing anxiety is an ongoing process. It's normal to have setbacks, but each setback is an opportunity to learn and grow. With practice and patience, you can become increasingly adept at navigating the challenges that anxiety presents.

In the next chapter, we'll discuss the importance of self-care and how it contributes to your overall well-being. Your journey towards embracing calm continues, and with each step, you're cultivating greater resilience and inner peace.

Embracing Calm: A Guide to Managing Anxiety

Chapter 7: The Vital Role of Self-Care

As we continue our journey towards managing anxiety and embracing a life of greater calm, we arrive at a chapter dedicated to one of the most critical aspects of well-being: self-care. In the hustle and bustle of everyday life, it's easy to neglect ourselves, but self-care is not a luxury—it's a necessity. By prioritizing self-care, you can nurture your physical and emotional health, fostering resilience against the challenges that anxiety may bring.

Understanding Self-Care

Self-care is a holistic approach to taking care of your physical, mental, and emotional well-being. It's about recognizing your needs and actively engaging in practices that promote your health and happiness. Here are the key elements of self-care:

Physical Self-Care:

1. **Nutrition:** Maintain a balanced diet rich in nutrients, and stay hydrated. Good nutrition supports your physical and mental health.

2. **Exercise:** Engage in regular physical activity that you enjoy. Exercise releases endorphins, which can boost your mood and reduce anxiety.

3. **Sleep:** Prioritize quality sleep. A well-rested body and mind are better equipped to manage stress and anxiety.

4. **Hygiene:** Maintain personal hygiene routines to feel refreshed and confident.

Embracing Calm: A Guide to Managing Anxiety

Mental and Emotional Self-Care:

1. **Mindfulness and Meditation:** Practice mindfulness to stay present and reduce stress. Meditation can calm your mind and promote emotional well-being.

2. **Relaxation Techniques:** Engage in activities that relax you, such as reading, taking baths, or listening to soothing music.

3. **Therapy and Counseling:** Seek professional help if needed. Therapy can provide valuable tools for managing anxiety and improving mental health.

4. **Limit Stressors:** Identify and address sources of chronic stress in your life. This might involve setting boundaries or making lifestyle changes.

Social Self-Care:

1. **Connection:** Nurture relationships with friends and loved ones. Social support is a vital buffer against anxiety and stress.

2. **Setting Boundaries:** Learn to say no when necessary and set healthy boundaries in your relationships.

3. **Social Activities:** Engage in social activities that bring you joy and fulfillment. Spending time with loved ones can boost your mood.

Practical Self-Care Strategies

Now, let's explore some practical self-care strategies that you can incorporate into your daily life:

Embracing Calm: A Guide to Managing Anxiety

1. Create a Self-Care Routine: Establish a daily or weekly self-care routine that includes activities you enjoy and find rejuvenating. This could be as simple as taking a nature walk, practicing yoga, or enjoying a quiet cup of tea.

2. Practice Gratitude: Regularly take time to reflect on the things you're grateful for. Gratitude can shift your focus away from anxiety-inducing worries and toward the positive aspects of your life.

3. Digital Detox: Disconnect from screens regularly. Excessive screen time can contribute to stress and anxiety. Spend time in nature, read a physical book, or engage in face-to-face conversations.

4. Explore Hobbies: Rediscover or develop new hobbies and interests that bring you joy. Engaging in creative or enjoyable activities can be a powerful form of self-care.

5. Set Realistic Goals: Avoid overwhelming yourself with unrealistic expectations. Set achievable goals and celebrate your accomplishments, no matter how small.

6. Seek Support: Don't hesitate to reach out to friends, family, or a support group when you're feeling overwhelmed. Sharing your feelings can provide relief and connection.

7. Embrace Mindful Eating: Pay attention to your eating habits. Eat slowly, savor your meals, and listen to your body's hunger and fullness cues.

8. Prioritize Sleep: Create a calming bedtime routine that signals your body it's time to rest. Avoid stimulating activities close to bedtime, and create a comfortable sleep environment.

9. Cultivate Mindfulness: Incorporate mindfulness practices into your daily life. This can involve mindful eating, mindful walking, or simply taking a few minutes each day to be fully present in the moment.

10. Practice Self-Compassion: Treat yourself with kindness and understanding, especially in moments of difficulty or anxiety. Remember that you're human, and it's okay to have imperfections.

The Continual Journey

Self-care is not a one-time endeavor but a lifelong commitment to your well-being. As you explore self-care practices, you'll discover what works best for you and how to integrate them into your daily life. Remember that taking care of yourself is not selfish—it's a necessary foundation for managing anxiety and living a fulfilling life.

In the next chapter, we'll explore the concept of resilience further and discuss how to bounce back from setbacks. Your journey towards embracing calm continues, and with each step, you're cultivating greater well-being and strength.

Chapter 8: Bouncing Back from Setbacks

Life is a journey filled with ups and downs, and on this path to managing anxiety and embracing calm, setbacks are an inevitable part of the terrain. In this chapter, we'll explore the concept of resilience in greater depth and discuss practical strategies for bouncing back from setbacks with grace and determination.

Understanding Resilience

Resilience is the ability to adapt and bounce back from adversity, challenges, and setbacks. It's not about avoiding difficulties but about facing them with courage and the belief that you can overcome them. Resilience is a quality that can be nurtured and strengthened over time. Here are key aspects of resilience:

1. Emotional Resilience: The capacity to manage and recover from emotional distress, such as anxiety, grief, or disappointment.

2. Problem-Solving: The ability to assess challenges objectively and find effective solutions.

3. Positive Outlook: Maintaining a hopeful and optimistic perspective, even in the face of adversity.

4. Support System: Utilizing social support and seeking help when needed.

5. Adaptability: Being flexible and open to change, even when it's uncomfortable.

6. Self-Compassion: Treating oneself with kindness and understanding, especially during difficult times.

Embracing Calm: A Guide to Managing Anxiety

Strategies for Building Resilience

Now, let's delve into practical strategies for building and strengthening resilience in your life:

1. Develop a Support System:

- Cultivate a network of friends and loved ones you can turn to in times of need.

- Seek professional help if required. Therapists, counselors, and support groups can provide valuable guidance and support.

2. Embrace Change:

- Understand that change is a natural part of life. Embrace it as an opportunity for growth.

- Learn to adapt to new circumstances and challenges. Flexibility is a key component of resilience.

3. Set Realistic Goals:

- Establish clear and achievable goals. Break larger goals into smaller, manageable steps.

- Celebrate your successes along the way, no matter how small they may seem.

4. Develop Problem-Solving Skills:

- When facing challenges, assess the situation objectively. What are the facts?

- Brainstorm potential solutions and choose the most practical and effective one.

- Implement your chosen solution and evaluate its effectiveness. Adjust if necessary.

5. Cultivate a Positive Outlook:

- Practice gratitude regularly. Focus on the positive aspects of your life, even in difficult times.

- Challenge negative thought patterns and replace them with more optimistic ones.

- Develop a sense of purpose and meaning in your life. Having a sense of direction can provide motivation and resilience.

6. Self-Care and Stress Management:

- Prioritize self-care practices that support your physical and emotional well-being.

- Engage in stress management techniques such as deep breathing, meditation, or progressive muscle relaxation.

7. Learn from Setbacks:

- View setbacks as opportunities for learning and growth. What can you take away from this experience?

- Avoid self-blame or dwelling on past mistakes. Instead, focus on moving forward with newfound wisdom.

8. Cultivate Self-Compassion:

- Treat yourself with the same kindness and understanding that you would offer a friend facing a similar situation.

- Acknowledge that it's okay to struggle at times. Self-compassion fosters resilience.

9. Seek Inspiration and Role Models:

- Explore stories of individuals who have overcome adversity. Their experiences can serve as a source of inspiration.

- Identify role models who exhibit resilience and learn from their coping strategies.

10. Maintain a Healthy Lifestyle:

- Continue to prioritize physical health through nutrition, exercise, and sleep.

- A healthy body is better equipped to cope with stress and adversity.

11. Stay Connected:

- Nurture your social connections and lean on your support system when needed.

- Share your feelings and experiences with trusted friends or family members.

Coping with Setbacks

Setbacks are a natural part of life, and how you respond to them can shape your resilience. Here's a step-by-step approach to coping with setbacks:

1. Allow Yourself to Feel: It's okay to feel a range of emotions, including sadness, frustration, or disappointment. Allow yourself to acknowledge and express these emotions.

2. Seek Support: Reach out to your support system for understanding and comfort. Sharing your feelings with someone you trust can provide relief.

3. Reframe Your Perspective: Challenge negative thought patterns and replace them with more constructive ones. Consider what you can learn from the setback.

4. Take Small Steps: Break down the process of recovery into manageable steps. Focus on taking one step at a time.

5. Practice Self-Compassion: Be gentle with yourself during this time. Avoid self-criticism or harsh judgments.

6. Stay Patient: Healing and recovery take time. Be patient with yourself as you navigate through the challenges.

7. Maintain a Positive Outlook: Keep your sights on the future and maintain hope that things will improve. Optimism is a powerful ally in building resilience.

8. Learn and Grow: View setbacks as opportunities for personal growth and development. What can you take away from this experience that will make you stronger?

Resilience is not about never experiencing setbacks; it's about bouncing back from them with greater strength and wisdom. As you continue your journey towards embracing calm, remember that each setback is a chance to grow and develop the resilience you need to face future challenges.

In the next chapter, we'll explore the importance of maintaining a sense of balance in your life and how it contributes to your overall well-being. Your journey continues, and with each step, you're cultivating greater inner strength.

Chapter 9: Finding Balance in Life

In this chapter, we'll explore the crucial concept of balance in life. Achieving balance is a vital component of managing anxiety and fostering overall well-being. Life can often feel like a juggling act, but by striving for balance, you can create a sense of harmony that supports your journey towards a calmer and more fulfilling existence.

What Is Balance?

Balance is about finding equilibrium in the various aspects of your life. It's recognizing that your well-being is influenced by multiple factors, and nurturing these areas can lead to a more harmonious and less anxiety-prone life. Here are the key dimensions of balance:

1. Work-Life Balance: Balancing your professional and personal life to avoid burnout and maintain a fulfilling personal life.

2. Physical and Mental Health: Caring for your physical well-being, including exercise, nutrition, and sleep, as well as nurturing your mental and emotional health.

3. Social Connections: Fostering meaningful relationships and maintaining social support networks.

4. Personal Growth: Continuously seeking opportunities for self-improvement, learning, and personal development.

5. Leisure and Relaxation: Incorporating downtime and enjoyable activities into your routine to recharge and de-stress.

6. Contribution and Purpose: Engaging in activities that provide a sense of purpose and contribute positively to your community or the world at large.

Strategies for Achieving Balance

Now, let's explore practical strategies for achieving balance in these key dimensions of your life:

1. Prioritize Self-Care:

- Set aside dedicated time for self-care activities that nurture your physical and emotional well-being.

- Ensure you get enough sleep, engage in regular exercise, and maintain a balanced diet.

2. Time Management:

- Efficiently manage your time to allocate it to work, personal life, relaxation, and personal growth.

- Use time management techniques like creating schedules or to-do lists to help you stay organized.

3. Boundaries:

- Set clear boundaries to prevent over commitment and burnout in both personal and professional spheres.

- Communicate your boundaries to others to ensure they are respected.

4. Quality over Quantity:

- Prioritize quality interactions and experiences over the quantity of activities or connections.

- Cultivate deep and meaningful relationships rather than spreading yourself too thin.

5. Mindfulness and Presence:

- Practice mindfulness to stay present in the moment and fully engage in your daily activities.

- Avoid multitasking, which can lead to increased stress and decreased focus.

6. Self-Reflection:

- Regularly assess your life's balance. Are there areas that need more attention or adjustment?

- Reflect on your priorities and values to ensure they align with your actions.

7. Learn to Say No:

- Don't be afraid to decline commitments or requests that may disrupt your balance.

- Saying no when necessary is a form of self-care and boundary-setting.

8. Set Achievable Goals:

- Set realistic and achievable goals in all areas of your life.

- Break larger goals into smaller, manageable steps to avoid feeling overwhelmed.

9. Embrace Leisure and Enjoyment:

- Schedule leisure and relaxation time into your routine.

- Engage in activities you enjoy and that bring you a sense of fulfillment and joy.

10. Seek Meaning and Purpose:

Reflect on your values and what gives your life meaning. - Explore activities or opportunities that align with your sense of purpose and contribute to your community or the world.

11. Seek Professional Help:

If anxiety or life imbalances are overwhelming, consider seeking the guidance of a therapist or counselor. - Professionals can provide tailored strategies to help you regain balance.

The Benefits of Balance

Achieving balance in life offers numerous benefits for managing anxiety and fostering well-being:

- **Reduced Stress:** A balanced life is less susceptible to the negative effects of chronic stress.

- **Improved Physical Health:** Prioritizing physical well-being leads to better health and increased resilience.

- **Enhanced Emotional Well-Being:** Balance supports mental and emotional health, reducing the likelihood of anxiety.

- **Stronger Relationships:** Quality time spent with loved ones strengthens social connections.

- **Increased Resilience:** Balance equips you with the tools to bounce back from setbacks more effectively.

Striving for Balance

Balancing the various aspects of your life is an ongoing process. Life is dynamic, and your needs and priorities may evolve over time. The key is to remain adaptable and attuned to your inner needs. Strive for balance, and remember that it's not about achieving perfection but about nurturing the different facets of your life to create a sense of harmony.

In the final chapter of this journey, we'll discuss the importance of embracing change and how it can lead to personal growth and lasting calm. Your journey continues, and with each step, you're cultivating greater inner strength and well-being.

Chapter 10: Embracing Change for Lasting Calm

As we embark on the final chapter of our journey towards managing anxiety and fostering a life of lasting calm, we delve into the profound concept of embracing change. Change is an inherent part of life, and by learning to accept and adapt to it, you can find greater resilience, growth, and inner peace.

The Nature of Change

Change is a constant in life, and it can manifest in various forms—both anticipated and unexpected. Whether it's a change in circumstances, relationships, or personal growth, how we navigate these transitions can significantly impact our overall well-being. Here are some key aspects to consider:

1. Inevitability: Change is a natural part of the human experience. It's unavoidable and can happen at any moment.

2. Resistance: It's common to resist change due to fear of the unknown or attachment to the familiar. However, resisting change can lead to anxiety and stress.

3. Adaptability: The ability to adapt to change is a valuable skill. It involves flexibility, openness, and the willingness to learn and grow.

4. Opportunity: Change presents opportunities for personal growth, new experiences, and a fresh perspective on life.

Strategies for Embracing Change

Now, let's explore practical strategies for embracing change with grace and resilience:

Embracing Calm: A Guide to Managing Anxiety

1. Mindful Awareness:

- Practice mindfulness to stay present and open to change.

- Recognize and acknowledge your emotions and thoughts regarding the change without judgment.

2. Reframe Your Perspective:

- Shift your mindset from viewing change as a threat to seeing it as an opportunity for growth.

- Focus on the potential positive outcomes and lessons that may come from change.

3. Acceptance:

- Accept that change is a natural part of life. Avoid resisting or fighting against it.

- Embrace the idea that some things are beyond your control, and that's okay.

4. Self-Care:

- Prioritize self-care practices during times of change to support your physical and emotional well-being.

- Self-care provides a stable foundation from which to navigate change.

5. Seek Support:

- Reach out to your support system—friends, family, or a therapist—when facing significant changes.

- Sharing your feelings and experiences can provide comfort and perspective.

6. Set Realistic Expectations:

- Understand that change may bring challenges and discomfort, but it's also an opportunity for growth.

- Set realistic expectations for yourself during times of transition.

7. Learn and Adapt:

- Embrace change as a chance to learn and adapt. Consider what new skills or knowledge you can gain from the experience.

- Reflect on past changes and how they've contributed to your personal growth.

8. Stay Positive:

- Maintain a positive outlook, even when facing uncertainty.

- Cultivate optimism by focusing on the aspects of change that align with your values and goals.

9. Flexibility:

- Develop the ability to be flexible and open to new possibilities.

- Be willing to adjust your plans and expectations as circumstances evolve.

10. Embrace Your Resilience:

Recognize that you have the inner strength and resilience to navigate change. - Trust in your ability to adapt and thrive in the face of life's transitions.

Change as a Catalyst for Growth

Change, even when challenging, is a catalyst for personal growth and transformation. It propels us out of our comfort zones and forces us to evolve, learn, and adapt. By embracing change with an open heart and a willingness to explore its possibilities, you can experience profound personal development and lasting calm.

Your Journey Continues

As we conclude this journey towards managing anxiety and embracing lasting calm, remember that life is an ongoing process of growth and self-discovery. You now possess a toolkit of strategies, insights, and practices to help you navigate the complexities of life with greater resilience and inner peace.

Embrace each day as a new opportunity to apply what you've learned, and know that the path to lasting calm is a continual journey. By practicing self-compassion, nurturing your well-being, building resilience, finding balance, and embracing change, you can create a life filled with calm, purpose, and fulfillment.

Thank you for joining me on this transformative journey. May you continue to cultivate the inner strength and serenity to face life's challenges with grace and courage.

With heartfelt wishes for your well-being and inner calm,

Ren Howard,

Author of "Embracing Calm: A Guide to Managing Anxiety"

Howard Advantage Solutions - 2023

Embracing Calm: A Guide to Managing Anxiety

Appendices: Additional Resources and Exercises for Your Journey

As you continue your journey towards managing anxiety and fostering lasting calm, I'm delighted to provide you with this collection of appendices. These resources and exercises are designed to further enhance your understanding and practice of the strategies discussed throughout this book. They serve as valuable companions on your path to well-being.

Appendix A: Guided Relaxation and Meditation

Audio and video resources are intended to help you develop and deepen your mindfulness practice, which is a powerful tool for managing anxiety and achieving inner calm. Whether you're new to meditation or a seasoned practitioner, these resources offer a range of options to suit your needs.

1. **Mindful Breathing Exercise:** A simple yet effective practice to bring your focus to the present moment and calm racing thoughts.

2. **Body Scan Meditation:** A guided meditation to help you release tension and stress by mindfully scanning your body.

3. **Loving-Kindness Meditation:** A meditation focused on cultivating feelings of compassion and love, both for yourself and others.

4. **Nature Visualization:** A guided visualization exercise to transport your mind to a peaceful natural setting.

5. **Progressive Muscle Relaxation:** A relaxation technique that involves systematically tensing and releasing muscle groups to reduce physical tension.

Embracing Calm: A Guide to Managing Anxiety

Appendix B: Recommended Reading

Books have the power to provide deeper insights and guidance on your journey towards managing anxiety and fostering lasting calm. This shortlist offers a selection of recommended reading materials, each chosen for its relevance to anxiety management, mindfulness, resilience, and personal development. These books can serve as companions for further exploration and learning.

1. **"The Anxiety and Phobia Workbook" by Edmund J. Bourne, PhD**

   - *Focus:* A comprehensive guide to understanding and managing anxiety, including practical exercises and techniques.

2. **"Wherever You Go, There You Are" by Jon Kabat-Zinn**

   - *Focus:* An introduction to mindfulness meditation and its potential to reduce anxiety and enhance well-being.

3. **"The Gifts of Imperfection" by Brené Brown**

   - *Focus:* Exploring vulnerability, courage, and self-compassion as tools for personal growth and resilience.

4. **"The Mindful Way Through Depression" by Mark Williams, John Teasdale, Zindel Segal, and Jon Kabat-Zinn**

   - *Focus:* Applying mindfulness-based cognitive therapy to manage and prevent depression and anxiety.

5. **"The Power of Now" by Eckhart Tolle**

- *Focus:* A spiritual guide to living in the present moment and reducing anxiety through mindfulness.

6. **"Radical Acceptance" by Tara Brach**

   - *Focus:* Embracing self-compassion and self-acceptance as a path to overcoming anxiety and finding inner peace.

7. **"Daring Greatly" by Brené Brown**

   - *Focus:* Exploring vulnerability, courage, and resilience in the face of anxiety and shame.

8. **"The Anxiety Toolkit" by Alice Boyes, PhD**

   - *Focus:* Practical strategies and tools for managing anxiety, including cognitive-behavioral techniques.

9. **"The Relaxation and Stress Reduction Workbook" by Martha Davis, Elizabeth Robbins Eshelman, and Matthew McKay**

   - *Focus:* A comprehensive resource for relaxation techniques and stress reduction strategies.

10. **"The Four Agreements" by Don Miguel Ruiz**

    - *Focus:* A guide to personal freedom and self-transformation by embracing four simple agreements, including "Don't Take Anything Personally."

These books offer valuable insights, practical techniques, and inspiration for your journey towards managing anxiety and promoting well-being. Depending on your specific interests and needs, you may find some resonate with you more than others. Take your time exploring these resources, and consider incorporating them into your reading list as you continue your path towards lasting calm.

Appendix C: Self-Care Toolkit

Self-care is an essential aspect of managing anxiety and promoting well-being. This toolkit provides a collection of self-care practices and activities that can empower you to prioritize your physical and emotional health. From self-care routines to journaling prompts and relaxation techniques, these tools are designed to support your well-being.

1. **Daily Self-Care Planner:** Helps you plan and track your daily self-care activities.

2. **Gratitude Journal:** A journaling tool to cultivate a positive mindset by reflecting on the things you're grateful for.

3. **Self-Compassion Exercise:** A guided exercise to practice self-compassion and self-kindness.

4. **Stress Reduction Techniques:** A compilation of relaxation exercises, including deep breathing and progressive muscle relaxation.

5. **Personal Growth Journal:** A journaling guide to explore your goals, values, and personal growth journey.

Appendix D: Support and Therapy Resources

Seeking professional support and guidance can be a crucial step in managing anxiety and fostering lasting calm. This appendix provides information and resources to help you connect with therapists, counselors, and support groups in your area. Whether you prefer in-person or online services, these resources can assist you in finding the help you need.

1. Finding a Therapist or Counselor:

- **Psychology Today:** This widely-used online directory allows you to search for therapists and counselors in your area based on your specific needs, preferences, and insurance coverage. Website: www.psychologytoday.com

- **GoodTherapy:** GoodTherapy provides a directory of mental health professionals, along with educational articles and resources to help you make an informed choice. Website: www.goodtherapy.org

2. Support Groups:

- **NAMI (National Alliance on Mental Illness):** NAMI offers a nationwide network of support groups for individuals and families affected by mental health conditions. Find a local chapter on their website. Website: www.nami.org

- **Meetup:** Meetup is an online platform that connects people with common interests, including mental health support groups. Search for local mental health support groups in your area. Website: www.meetup.com

3. Online Therapy Platforms:

- **BetterHelp:** BetterHelp offers convenient online therapy and counseling services, connecting you with licensed therapists via text, audio, or video messaging. Website: www.betterhelp.com

- **Talkspace:** Talkspace provides online therapy and counseling through messaging, as well as video sessions. Their platform offers flexibility in accessing professional support. Website: www.talkspace.com

4. Teletherapy Platforms:

- **Teladoc Health:** Teladoc Health offers telehealth services, including virtual therapy sessions with licensed therapists. Check with your healthcare provider or insurance for coverage options. Website: www.teladochealth.com

- **Amwell:** Amwell provides access to licensed therapists and mental health professionals through secure video sessions, making it easier to receive therapy from the comfort of your home. Website: www.amwell.com

5. University Counseling Centers:

- **If you are a student, your university or college likely offers counseling services to students. Contact your campus counseling center for information on available resources and support.**

Please note that the availability of in-person and online therapy services may vary based on your location and individual circumstances. It's essential to research and consider your options to find the best fit for your needs and preferences.

Remember that seeking help is a courageous and proactive step towards managing anxiety and promoting your well-being. Whether you choose individual therapy, group support, or online counseling, professional guidance can provide valuable tools and strategies to navigate life's challenges.

Appendix E: Worksheets and Exercises

Practical exercises and worksheets can aid in implementing the strategies discussed in this book. Google has an array of downloadable and printable resources to assist you in setting goals, tracking progress, and gaining deeper insights into your thoughts and emotions.

1. **Goal Setting Worksheet:** A tool to help you set and track your anxiety management goals.

2. **Thought Journal:** A template for recording and analyzing your thoughts to identify patterns.

3. **Emotion Regulation Worksheet:** A resource to explore and manage your emotions effectively.

4. **Anxiety Coping Strategies:** A compilation of coping strategies to use during moments of anxiety.

5. **Values Clarification Exercise:** A guide to help you identify and prioritize your core values.

Appendix F: Mobile Apps and Online Resources

In today's digital age, mobile apps offer convenient tools and resources for managing anxiety, promoting mindfulness, and fostering well-being. This appendix provides a list of recommended apps, each designed to support various aspects of mental health, relaxation, and personal growth. Whether you're seeking guided meditation, stress reduction, or tools for self-care, these apps can be valuable companions on your journey towards lasting calm.

1. Calm

- **Focus:** Guided meditation, sleep stories, and relaxation exercises.

- **Key Features:** Daily calm sessions, breathing exercises, and sleep stories for better rest.

2. Headspace

- **Focus:** Meditation, mindfulness, and stress reduction.

- **Key Features:** Guided meditation sessions, mindfulness practices, and sleep aid exercises.

3. Insight Timer

- **Focus:** Meditation, relaxation, and personal growth.

- **Key Features:** A vast library of guided meditations, music, and talks by mindfulness experts.

4. 10% Happier

- **Focus:** Mindfulness, meditation, and personal development.

- **Key Features:** Guided meditation courses and interviews with meditation teachers.

5. Waking Up with Sam Harris

- **Focus:** Mindfulness, meditation, and philosophy.

- **Key Features:** Daily guided meditations and lessons on consciousness and well-being.

6. Smiling Mind

- **Focus:** Mindfulness and well-being for all ages.

- **Key Features:** Mindfulness programs tailored to different age groups, including children and adults.

7. Breathe2Relax

- **Focus:** Stress management through diaphragmatic breathing.

- **Key Features:** Guided breathing exercises to reduce stress and anxiety.

8. MyLife Meditation (formerly Stop, Breathe & Think)

- **Focus:** Mindfulness, meditation, and emotional well-being.

- **Key Features:** Customized meditation recommendations based on your emotional state.

9. Daylio

- **Focus:** Mood tracking, self-care, and emotional awareness.

- **Key Features:** Daily mood and activity tracking for greater self-awareness.

Appendix G: Crisis and Helpline Contacts

During challenging times, reaching out for immediate assistance and support is essential. This appendix provides contact information for crisis and helpline services that are available to offer help, guidance, and a listening ear when you need it most. Please remember that you don't have to face difficult moments alone, and there are trained professionals ready to assist you.

National Crisis Helplines:

1. **National Suicide Prevention Lifeline:**

   - Phone: 1-800-273-TALK (1-800-273-8255)

- Website: www.suicidepreventionlifeline.org

The National Suicide Prevention Lifeline provides 24/7 confidential support for individuals in crisis, including those struggling with thoughts of suicide or emotional distress.

2. **Crisis Text Line:**

- Text "HOME" to 741741

- Website: www.crisistextline.org

Crisis Text Line offers free, confidential text-based support for individuals experiencing emotional crisis. Trained crisis counselors are available 24/7 to provide assistance.

3. **National Domestic Violence Hotline:**

- Phone: 1-800-799-SAFE (1-800-799-7233)

- Website: www.thehotline.org

The National Domestic Violence Hotline offers support, safety planning, and resources for individuals affected by domestic violence or abuse.

Specialized Helplines:

4. **Veterans Crisis Line:**

- Phone: 1-800-273-8255 (Press 1 for veterans)

- Website: www.veteranscrisisline.net

The Veterans Crisis Line provides support for veterans and service members in crisis, offering confidential assistance 24/7.

5. **Substance Abuse and Mental Health Services Administration (SAMHSA) National Helpline:**

- Phone: 1-800-662-HELP (1-800-662-4357)

- Website: www.samhsa.gov/find-help/national-helpline

SAMHSA's National Helpline offers information, referrals, and support for individuals and families facing substance use and mental health challenges.

6. **LGBT National Help Center:**

- Phone: 1-888-843-4564

- Website: www.glbthotline.org

The LGBT National Help Center provides support and resources to LGBTQ+ individuals, including a confidential hotline.

7. **National Eating Disorders Association (NEDA) Helpline:**

- Phone: 1-800-931-2237

- Website: www.nationaleatingdisorders.org/help-support/contact-helpline

NEDA's Helpline offers support and information for individuals and loved ones affected by eating disorders.

Please remember that these crisis and helpline services are here to provide assistance and support when you're going through difficult times. You don't have to face your challenges alone, and seeking help is a sign of strength. If you or someone you know is in immediate danger or experiencing a life-threatening emergency, please call 911 or your local emergency services.

With the support of these helplines and the resources in this book, may you find the strength and guidance to navigate challenging moments and continue your journey towards lasting calm and well-being.

Appendix H: Notes and Journaling

Journaling can be a powerful practice for self-reflection, emotional processing, personal reflections, insights, and notes as you progress through your journey.

Appendix I: Terms and Definitions

Understanding the terminology related to anxiety management and well-being is essential for effective communication and comprehension. In this appendix, you'll find a glossary of key terms and definitions that are frequently used throughout this book and in the field of mental health. Familiarizing yourself with these terms will enhance your understanding of the concepts discussed.

1. **Anxiety:** A natural and adaptive response to stress or perceived threats. Anxiety becomes a concern when it is excessive, prolonged, or interferes with daily life.

2. **Coping Strategies:** Techniques and behaviors used to manage and reduce the impact of anxiety and stress.

3. **Resilience:** The ability to adapt, recover, and bounce back from adversity, stress, or challenges.

4. **Mindfulness:** A mental practice involving paying deliberate attention to the present moment without judgment. It promotes self-awareness and reduces rumination.

5. **Stress:** The body's physiological and psychological response to perceived threats or demands, often accompanied by physical or emotional tension.

6. **Relaxation Techniques:** Methods used to induce a state of relaxation, including deep breathing, progressive muscle relaxation, and guided imagery.

7. **Self-Care:** The practice of actively taking steps to maintain and improve one's physical, emotional, and mental well-being.

8. **Self-Compassion:** Treating oneself with kindness, understanding, and acceptance, especially in times of difficulty or failure.

9. **Mindset:** A set of beliefs, attitudes, and thought patterns that influence one's perception of self, others, and the world.

10. **Triggers:** Events, situations, or stimuli that initiate or exacerbate feelings of anxiety or stress.

11. **Social Support:** The network of friends, family, and peers who provide emotional, practical, and moral support during challenging times.

12. **Cognitive Behavioral Therapy (CBT):** A psychotherapy approach that focuses on identifying and changing negative thought patterns and behaviors contributing to anxiety and other mental health issues.

13. **Mind-Body Connection:** The relationship between mental and emotional well-being and physical health.

14. **Wellness:** A holistic concept encompassing physical, emotional, social, and mental well-being.

15. **Resilience Building:** The process of developing and strengthening the ability to cope with adversity and stress.

16. **Emotional Intelligence:** The capacity to recognize, understand, manage, and express emotions effectively, both in oneself and in others.

17. **Self-Reflection:** The practice of introspection and examining one's thoughts, feelings, and behaviors for personal growth and self-improvement.

18. **Crisis Helpline:** A telephone service providing immediate support and assistance during times of emotional or psychological crisis.

19. **Meditation:** A mental practice that involves focused attention and awareness to cultivate relaxation, clarity, and mindfulness.

20. **Mindfulness-Based Stress Reduction (MBSR):** A structured program incorporating mindfulness meditation to reduce stress and improve well-being.

21. **Therapist:** A trained and licensed mental health professional who provides counseling and therapy services.

22. **Teletherapy:** The provision of therapy and counseling services through remote means, typically using online video or phone calls.

23. **Progressive Muscle Relaxation (PMR):** A relaxation technique involving the systematic tensing and releasing of muscle groups to reduce physical tension.

24. **Cognitive Distortions:** Inaccurate and irrational thought patterns that can contribute to anxiety and stress.

25. **Values Clarification:** The process of identifying and prioritizing one's core values, which guide decision-making and actions.

These definitions provide a foundation for understanding the concepts and strategies discussed in this book. As you delve deeper into your journey towards managing anxiety and fostering lasting calm, these terms will serve as valuable reference points.

Appendix J: Acknowledgments

I'd like to take a moment to express my gratitude to all those who have contributed to the creation of this book. Your support, insights, and encouragement have played a significant role in bringing this project to life. Thank you for being a part of this journey towards managing anxiety and embracing lasting calm.

Thank you for embarking on this transformative journey towards managing anxiety and fostering lasting calm. May these appendices serve as valuable companions on your path to well-being.

Made in the USA
Columbia, SC
16 September 2023

22923934R10035